Sports Illustrated KIDS

Car Racing GOATs

The Greatest Athletes of All Time

BY BRENDAN FLYNN

CAPSTONE PRESS
a capstone imprint

Published by Capstone Press, an imprint of Capstone
1710 Roe Crest Drive, North Mankato, Minnesota 56003
capstonepub.com

Copyright © 2024 by Capstone. All rights reserved. No part of this publication may be reproduced in whole or in part, or stored in a retrieval system, or transmitted in any form or by any means, electronic, mechanical, photocopying, recording, or otherwise, without written permission of the publisher.

SPORTS ILLUSTRATED KIDS is a trademark of ABG-SI LLC. Used with permission.

Library of Congress Cataloging-in-Publication Data is available
on the Library of Congress website.

ISBN: 9781669062943 (hardcover)
ISBN: 9781669063049 (paperback)
ISBN: 9781669062981 (ebook PDF)

Summary: How do you pick car racing's GOATs? Richard Petty and Jeff Gordon get a lot of attention. But what about NHRA champion Brittany Force? And what about the versatile driver A.J. Foyt? It comes down to stats, history, and hunches. Read more about some of the legends of car racing and see if you agree that they're the greatest of all time.

Editorial Credits
Editor: Ericka Smith; Designer: Sarah Bennett; Media Researcher: Svetlana Zhurkin; Production Specialist: Katy LaVigne

Image Credits
Associated Press: 19, 25 (top), Autostock/Nigel Kinrade, cover (bottom middle), Bob Galbraith, 21, Icon Sportswire/LVMS/Jeff Speer, cover (top right); Getty Images: Allsport/David Taylor, 6, 10, Allsport/Pascal Rondeau, 29, CQ-Roll Call Group/ISC Archives, 26, 27 (bottom), Jared C. Tilton, 5, Klemantaski Collection/Bill Fox, 16, Mark Thompson, 12, 13, 14, NASCAR/Jason Smith, 9, NASCAR/Tom Whitmore, 8, Pool/Tolga Bozoglu, 15, Sports Illustrated/George Tiedemann, 7, Streeter Lecka, 27 (top), The Enthusiast Network/Bob D'Olivo, 20, The Enthusiast Network/Mike Brenner, 25 (bottom), Tribune News Service/Belleville News-Democrat/Zia Nizami, 22; Newscom: Icon Sportswire/LVMS/Jeff Speer, 23, National Motor Museum Heritage Images, 17 (top); Shutterstock: Apostle (star background), cover and throughout, Bruce Alan Bennett, 17 (bottom), cristiano barni, cover (top left), Grindstone Media Group, 11, Sunward Art (star confetti), 4 and throughout; Sports Illustrated: Heinz Kluetmeier, cover (bottom left), Simon Bruty, cover (top middle and bottom right)

All internet sites appearing in back matter were available and accurate when this book was sent to press.

Direct Quotation
Page 24, from Sept. 4, 2022, *Sports History Weekly* article "Don Garlits, Godfather of American Drag Racing," sportshistoryweekly.com

All records and statistics in this book are current through 2022.

Printed and bound in China. 6667

Table of Contents

Words in **bold** appear in the glossary.

How to Pick Car Racing's Greatest?

A group of cars zooms through the final turn of a race. They speed toward the finish line. The checkered flag flaps wildly as the cars cross the line. The winner pumps their fist, and their team celebrates on pit row. Another victory adds to the driver's legend.

Today, fans can watch drivers race different types of cars for prizes and fame. In NASCAR, drivers race colorful, speedy stock cars on huge oval courses. IndyCar and Formula 1 (F1) racers drive sleek, high-tech cars with huge wheels. Some races are on oval tracks. Others are on road courses that zigzag through cities. And drag racing features powerful cars that go super-fast in a straight line.

Each type of race requires different skills. So how do you pick the greatest drivers of all time? The best drivers are aggressive, daring, and confident.

xfinity
GRAGSON
Bass Pro Shops
MRN

NASCAR

Dale Earnhardt

Dale Earnhardt was known as "The Intimidator." Other drivers feared the sight of his black car in their rearview mirrors. He was known for bumping others out of the way and zooming past them.

In 1980, Earnhardt won his first NASCAR season championship. Then he went on to win six more. He won four of them between 1990 and 1994.

Earnhardt competing in the 1995 NASCAR NAPA 500

But the race Earnhardt wanted to win the most—the Daytona 500—escaped him for years. In 1998, Earnhardt finally won his first Daytona 500. The other drivers and their **pit crews** lined up to congratulate him after the race. They wanted to show their respect for one of NASCAR's greatest drivers.

Earnhardt isn't the only Daytona 500 winner in his family. In 2004, his son, Dale Earnhardt Jr., won the Daytona 500—just six years after his father's win.

Sadly, Earnhardt was killed when his car crashed in the final turn of the 2001 Daytona 500. But his death led to many safety improvements that have protected other drivers since the accident.

Jimmie Johnson

Jimmie Johnson grew up racing motorcycles. But his biggest victories came behind the wheel of a stock car. He made his **debut** in NASCAR's top series in 2001. The next year, he won three races and finished fifth in the final standings. The talent he showed on the track his second year in NASCAR was a sign of things to come.

For the next 18 years, Johnson was one of NASCAR's most strategic—and successful—drivers. He would play it safe for most of a race and push to the front at the end. That plan worked well for Johnson. He won seven NASCAR season championships, including five straight wins between 2006 and 2010. No other driver has ever had a more **dominating** stretch in NASCAR history.

Johnson crosses the finish line to win the 2010 NASCAR Sprint Cup Series.

Johnson celebrates after winning the 2010 NASCAR Sprint Cup Series.

Most NASCAR Season Championships

Driver	Number of Season Championships	Years
Jimmie Johnson	7	2006, 2007, 2008, 2009, 2010, 2013, 2016
Dale Earnhardt	7	1980, 1986, 1987, 1990, 1991, 1993, 1994
Richard Petty	7	1964, 1967, 1971, 1972, 1974, 1975, 1979
Jeff Gordon	4	1995, 1997, 1998, 2001

Jeff Gordon

As a Midwesterner among many Southerners, Jeff Gordon was often seen as an outsider by many NASCAR fans. But nobody could question his talent.

In 1995, the 24-year-old Gordon became the youngest driver to win the NASCAR season championship. He added three more titles by 2001. He also won the Daytona 500 three times and the Brickyard 400 a record five times.

Gordon competing in the NASCAR NAPA 500 in 1995

The clean-cut Gordon also drew new fans to NASCAR. They loved to cheer for him in his rainbow-colored car. He became one of the world's most famous sports figures. He even hosted *Saturday Night Live*.

When Gordon retired in 2016, he had 93 career victories. Only two other NASCAR drivers have won more races.

Formula 1

Michael Schumacher & Sebastian Vettel

Michael Schumacher and Sebastian Vettel are two of the best F1 drivers of all time. Schumacher's hunger to win every race led him to great heights. And Vettel's bold driving helped earn him some record achievements.

As a boy, Schumacher raced go-karts in Germany. By the time he was 22, he was racing F1 cars. Three years later, in 1994, he won his first F1 series championship. Schumacher dominated the sport, winning a total of seven championships. When he retired in 2006, he'd won a record 91 F1 races.

Schumacher competing in an F1 Grand Prix race in Shanghai, China, in 2006

Vettel crosses the finish line to win the Brazilian F1 Grand Prix race in 2013.

Vettel also grew up in Germany. He **idolized** Schumacher as a boy. He even raced go-karts like his hero did.

In 2007, Vettel made his F1 debut. At age 21, Vettel became the youngest driver to win an F1 race. Two years later, he became the youngest F1 series champion. It was the first of four straight championships for Vettel. He retired in 2022 with 53 wins.

Lewis Hamilton

As a young boy in England, Lewis Hamilton also enjoyed go-kart racing. When he was a teenager, Hamilton zoomed through the lower racing **circuits**. He made his F1 debut in 2007, two months after he turned 22. He became the first Black racer to drive at F1's highest level.

From the start, Hamilton showed the world he was one of its best drivers. As a **rookie**, he won an amazing four races. He tied the record set by Jacques Villeneuve in 1996. He was also in the running for the series championship the entire season.

In 2010, Lewis Hamilton won the Canadian F1 Grand Prix race for the second time.

Hamilton celebrates his 2020 World Drivers' Championship win in Istanbul, Turkey.

That was just the start for Hamilton. He won his first championship in 2008. Then, he won six titles in seven years, tying Michael Schumacher with his seventh in 2020. By 2024, he also topped Schumacher's record number of F1 wins. He had won 105 F1 races.

IndyCar

Al Unser Sr.

The most famous IndyCar race is the Indianapolis 500. And Al Unser Sr. is one of the best ever to win that race.

Between his debut in 1964 and his retirement in 1994, Unser won 39 IndyCar races. He excelled at the Indianapolis 500, which he won four times. No driver has won that race more times than Unser.

Unser competing in the 1971 Indianapolis 500, which would become his second win in that race

In 1978, Unser won the Indianapolis 500 for the third time.

In 1970, Unser edged out his brother Bobby to win the first of his three series championships. That was a big year for Unser. He won a stunning 10 races on the IndyCar circuit. In 1987, he became the oldest driver to win the Indianapolis 500, five days before his 48th birthday.

Unser came from a racing family. His father, uncles, and three brothers were professional racers too. Unser's son, several nephews, a niece, and even two grandsons followed in their footsteps.

Al Unser Jr.

A.J. Foyt

A.J. Foyt was a legend at the Indianapolis Motor Speedway. Foyt was the first driver to win the Indianapolis 500 four times. He is also the only driver ever to compete in the race for 35 **consecutive** years. Foyt's success at the "Brickyard" helped him set another record as well. He won seven series championships between 1960 and 1979.

The Houston, Texas, native was **versatile** too. He's the only driver to win the Indianapolis 500, the Daytona 500, and the 24 Hours of Le Mans. He won on road courses, dirt tracks, and paved ovals.

Foyt retired in 1993 with 67 career IndyCar victories under his belt. That's nine more than his nearest competitor.

Foyt celebrates his 1977 Indianapolis 500 win—his record-setting fourth win.

Mario Andretti

When Mario Andretti was a boy in Italy, he dreamed of racing cars. His dream became a reality after his family moved to the United States in 1955. Soon after their move, Andretti was racing all types of cars. But IndyCar races became his specialty.

In 1965, Andretti won his first IndyCar race. He also took third in his first Indianapolis 500 that year. He ended the season with his first series championship. The next year, he matched that **feat**, winning eight races in the process.

Andretti during his first Indianapolis 500 race in 1965

Andretti (right) and Paul Newman, one of the owners of his team, celebrate his 1987 Toyota Grand Prix win.

Andretti dabbled in other forms of racing too. In 1967, he won the Daytona 500. Later that year he won the 12 Hours of Sebring, an **endurance** race. And he won the F1 World Championship in 1978.

Andretti retired in 1994 with four IndyCar season titles and 52 race victories.

Andretti began racing cars with his identical twin Aldo. After a couple of serious accidents, Aldo stopped racing, but he stayed involved with the sport.

Drag Racing

John Force & Brittany Force

The story of drag racing cannot be told without mentioning the Force family. John Force was a bit of a **late bloomer** in the drag racing world. He didn't win a race in his first ten seasons on the National Hot Rod Association (NHRA) tour. But in 1987, he finally won his first event. He was 38 years old. He went on to win a record 16 NHRA season championships between 1990 and 2013.

John Force competing in an NHRA race in 2008

Brittany Force celebrates her win at the NHRA Four-Wide Nationals in 2022.

Force's daughters Courtney, Ashley, and Brittany also joined the family business. Brittany is the most successful of the three. In fact, she's one of the most successful female drivers of all time. She won an NHRA season championship in 2017. That made her the first woman in 35 years to win the title. And she repeated the feat in 2022.

Don Garlits

Don Garlits thought the formula for being a successful drag racer was rather simple. "You need to have extremely good reflexes and be very cool-headed," he said. However, Garlits was more than just quick and calm. Nicknamed "Big Daddy," he had a larger-than-life personality that matched his success on the track.

Garlits began drag racing in the early 1950s, when the sport was just starting to get organized. In 1955, he won his first official NHRA race at age 23.

But Garlits was just getting started. He went on to race for nearly 40 years. His "Swamp Rat" dragster was one of the most famous cars in the world. Together, they set numerous speed records. Garlits also won 144 national events and 17 season championships.

Garlits celebrates winning a 1968 drag racing competition.

Garlits driving Swamp Rat 14 in 1971

The All-Around Greatest

Richard Petty

Mention "the King" to any NASCAR fan, and they'll know which driver you're talking about—Richard Petty. Petty is considered the greatest stock car driver of all time.

The statistics make that clear enough. In 1959, Petty was named NASCAR's Rookie of the Year. In 1964, he won the first of seven Daytona 500s. He also won the season championship that year, an accomplishment he'd match six more times.

Petty competing in a race in 1967

Over his 34-year career, Petty won a record 200 NASCAR races. David Pearson is second, with just 105 victories!

But Petty was more than just a champion. He was a character. Known for his black cowboy hat, bushy mustache, and dark glasses, Petty was a popular figure everywhere he went.

The Petty Family

The Petty family's success wasn't limited to Richard. His father Lee was a legend in NASCAR's early days. Lee won the first Daytona 500 in 1959. He won a total of 54 career races, and he is a NASCAR Hall of Famer. Richard's son Kyle was also a successful NASCAR driver. He had eight wins and 173 top-10 finishes in his 30-year career.

Lee Petty

Ayrton Senna

Ayrton Senna's career was short but spectacular. Senna was known for reaching speeds others dared not attempt. He thrived in any weather. And his skill and fearlessness pushed him past his competition. It earned him fans around the world too.

As a kid in Brazil, Senna dreamed of racing F1 cars. He started racing go-karts at age 13. At the age of 24, he'd made his F1 debut.

Senna rose to the top of the sport quickly. Motivated by a rivalry with Alain Prost, Senna pushed himself to be the best. Between 1988 and 1994, he won 35 races and three F1 series championships.

Unfortunately, Senna's life was cut short in 1994. He was killed in a crash at a race in San Marino. But he died as he lived, pushing himself to the limit. And his commitment to the sport is one reason fans and drivers admire him to this day.

Senna celebrating after winning the Japanese F1 Grand Prix in 1993

Glossary

circuit (SUHR-kuht)—a series of races that leads to a single championship

consecutive (kuhn-SEK-yuh-tiv)—when something happens several times in a row without a break

debut (DAY-byoo)—a first appearance

dominate (DAH-muh-nayt)—to rule; in sports, a team or person dominates if they win much more than anyone else

endurance (en-DUR-uhns)—the ability to keep doing an activity for a long period of time

feat (FEET)—an achievement that requires great courage, skill, or strength

idolize (EYE-duh-lize)—to admire someone

late bloomer (LAYT BLOOM-er)—a person who finds initial success later than most

pit crew (PIT KROO)—a team of people who work with drivers to keep race cars in top shape

rookie (RUK-ee)—a first-year competitor

versatile (VUR-suh-tuhl)—talented or useful in many ways

Read More

Cain, Harold P. *Lewis Hamilton: Auto Racing Star.* Lake Elmo, MN: Focus Readers, 2023.

Flynn, Brendan. *Car Racing Records Smashed!* North Mankato, MN: Capstone, 2024.

Rule, Heather. *Ultimate NASCAR Road Trip.* Minneapolis: ABDO, 2019.

Internet Sites

Formula One
formula1.com

NASCAR
nascar.com

NHRA
nhra.com

Index

About the Author

Brendan Flynn is a San Francisco resident and an author of numerous children's books. In addition to writing about sports, Flynn also enjoys competing in triathlons, Scrabble tournaments, and chili cook-offs.